Gifted and Talented Children

A Planning Guide

Shirley Taylor

Jessica Kingsley Publishers
London and Philadelphia

First published in New Zealand in 2001 by
User Friendly Resource Enterprises Limited

This edition published in the United Kingdom in 2002 by
Jessica Kingsley Publishers Ltd
116 Pentonville Road
London N1 9JB, England
and
325 Chestnut Street
Philadelphia, PA 19106, USA

www.jkp.com

ACKNOWLEDGEMENTS

The publishers wish to acknowledge the work of the following people in the various stages of publishing this resource.

Designers: e2-media
Illustrators: Geraldine Sloane and Akira Le Fevre
Editor: Pauline Scanlan

Library of Congress Cataloging in Publication Data
A CIP catalog record for this book is available from the Library of Congress

British Library Cataloguing in Publication Data
A CIP record for this book is available from the British Library

ISBN 1 84310 086 X

Printed and Bound in Great Britain by
Athenaeum Press, Gateshead, Tyne and Wear

CONTENTS

INTRODUCTION 1

SECTION 1   **WHO ARE GIFTED AND TALENTED CHILDREN?** 2

SECTION 2   **WHAT ARE WE DOING? WHAT DO WE NEED TO DO?** 4

How to begin? 5

Thinking it through: using the questionnaire 9

Creative problem-solving 16

SECTION 3   **GETTING INTO SCHOOL-WIDE ACTION** 18

Identification in the school and classroom 18

Identification of abilities and needs 26

Learning needs and programming options 28

Evaluation 33

SECTION 4   **WHAT CAN WE DO IN THE CLASSROOM?** 35

Providing a responsive environment 35

Learning and teaching strategies 37

Specific examples of provisions in the classroom 45

Unit analysis and adaptation 49

Social/emotional development 51

Relating to parents 55

Conclusion 55

Recommended reading for children 57

REFERENCES 60

FURTHER READING 61

INTRODUCTION

Children who are gifted and talented are also referred to as children with special abilities (cwsa). These terms will be used interchangeably in this planning guide. They are not intended as labels but as descriptors. For example, a child who has a special ability in mathematics may be a child who has blue eyes, is the youngest child in her family, plays netball and likes singing. Her special ability describes one aspect (albeit important) of her as a person.

This planning guide has been written for primary school teachers, principals and support staff who have gifted and talented children in their school communites and who require some specific practical strategies to work effectively with these children. It is based on three ideas:

1. **That children with special abilities can be provided for in an inclusive school setting.** This means a setting where schools have a philosophy of responding to all abilities and needs, and where there are flexibilities in approaches to teaching and learning. This does not mean that everyone does the same thing in the same way or in the same place.

2. **That special abilities are broad ranging** and therefore a definition of giftedness is not narrow but wide and inclusive.

3. **That identification of and programming for giftedness are linked** and together underpin school policy.

The starting point in providing effectively for gifted and talented children in your school is looking at what you are doing now, as a school or as an individual.

The starting point in providing effectively for gifted and talented children in your school is looking at what you are doing now, as a school or as an individual. No doubt you are doing much already. By deciding where you are, personally and collectively, you will be able to develop a framework in the form of a written policy. This policy will provide consistency of provision. When this happens children with special abilities can have a good year every year, not just occasionally when their class teacher happens to have a particular interest in their needs.

The questionnaires in this guide will help you to focus on and analyse your practice collectively and individually and also to set targets for action. Strategies are also included for implementing school-wide and classroom practices.

Now is as good a time as any to make a concerted effort to focus on the needs of children with special abilities and give them joy in learning.

SECTION 1
WHO ARE GIFTED AND TALENTED CHILDREN?

▸ 6 year old *John* loves machines and gadgets; he wants to know how things work and has taken several tape recorders apart at home.

▸ *Kirsty* discovered debating when she was 11 years old and is the lead speaker in her team.

▸ 7 year old *Tom* hardly ever finishes work because he is always rubbing it out and starting over. His ideas don't seem to look as good to him on paper as they sounded in his head. His teacher says his work is fine but he is not satisfied.

▸ *Olive*, who is 5, does not get much written work done because she is always watching other people and taking in everything that is happening.

▸ 6 year old *Greta* pretends to like the picture books others are reading at school but at home reads long chapter books.

▸ 11 year old *Sharon* would love a real friend who thinks like her but hasn't found one yet. However she likes being alone; she can do the things she wants to do.

▸ 9 year old *William* challenged the teacher when another child was punished for not finishing work. William believed the work set was inappropriate.

▸ *Sarah* lies awake some nights worrying about war and the starving people she has seen on the TV news, though she is only 6 years old.

▸ 5 year old *Hing* gets totally absorbed in drawing and will not stop when his mother or his teacher want him to.

▸ *Fiona,* who is 4, knows the names of all the dinosaurs and can classify them by type and time periods.

▸ 7 year old *Mere* makes jokes that only the teacher can understand.

▸ 9 year old *Anna* only needs to hear a tune once and she can hum it or pick it out on the piano.

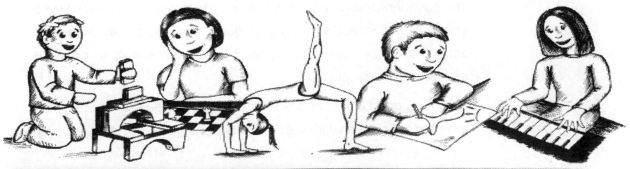

- 10 year old *Steve* hates fantasy books but loves the encyclopedia and factual books.

- *Lusi*, who is 8, suggested that the Venn diagram they had learnt about in maths could be used to consider what was the same and different about the societies they were studying for another unit, thus demonstrating transfer of learning.

- *Neil* is only interested in Egyptology and wants to go to Egypt. He is 7.

- *Marie* taught herself to read by the time she was 4.

- 10 year old *Linda* is the chess champion at her school and can now beat her mother and father.

- 3 year old *Craig* builds elaborate constructions out of blocks and won't let them be knocked down; he tells his parents and visitors all about them in detail.

- *Rawiri* is leader of the Kapa Haka group and makes speeches in Te Reo Maori to welcome visitors at school. He is 10 years of age.

- *Michelle*, who is 8, loves talking, problem-solving and art but has a specific learning difficulty with reading and writing.

- 12 year old *Fiona* is a deep thinker and knows her own strengths and weaknesses well; she self evaluates her work accurately.

- *Barbara*, who is 8, is on to advanced badge work in gymnastics.

> All of these children have special abilities but they are different from one another. Perhaps some of the children in your class have characteristics similar to the children profiled here.
>
> Defining special abilities or giftedness is discussed in the next section of this planning guide.

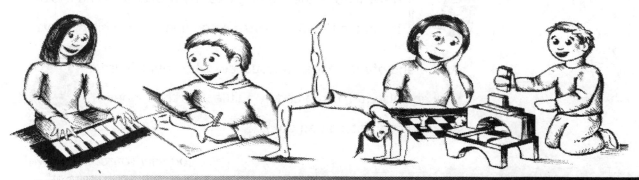

SECTION 2
WHAT ARE WE DOING? WHAT DO WE NEED TO DO?

The Fable of the Animal School

Once upon a time the animals decided that they must do something heroic to meet the problems of the new world. So they organised a school. They adopted an activity curriculum consisting of running, climbing, swimming and flying.

To make it easier to administer the curriculum, all the animals took all the subjects. The duck was excellent in swimming; in fact he was better than the instructor – but he made only passing grades in flying and was very poor in running. Since he was so slow in running he had to stay in after school and also had to drop swimming (in order to practise running). This was kept up until his webbed feet were badly worn and he was only average in swimming; but average is acceptable in school, so nobody worried about that except the duck.

The rabbit started at the top of the class in running but had a nervous breakdown because she had so much work to catch up with swimming.

The possum was excellent in climbing until she became frustrated in the flying class where her teacher made her start from the ground up instead of from the treetop down.

The eagle was a problem child and had to be severely disciplined. In the climbing class he beat all the others to the top of the tree but insisted on getting there in his own way.

At the end of the year an unusual eel who could swim well and also run, climb and fly a little, had the highest average and was named dux!

(original source unknown)

SECTION 2
What are we doing? What do we need to do?

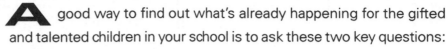
gifted and talented children: a planning guide

HOW TO BEGIN?

Start By Focusing

A good way to find out what's already happening for the gifted and talented children in your school is to ask these two key questions:

What are we doing already?

What else do we need to do?

Answering the first question is the most rewarding, so start there. Together as a staff, brainstorm everything you are doing already. Perhaps you are:

▸ holding workshops with local artists for those with special ability in art

▸ teaching thinking skills in each classroom

▸ having a science fair bi-annually

▸ using Bloom's taxonomy in planning.

Writing each of these provisions on separate pieces of paper is useful because you will see that it's possible to group them under two headings:

PROGRAMMING FOR ALL CHILDREN	DIFFERENTIATION ACCORDING TO NEEDS OF CHILDREN WITH SPECIAL ABILITIES

If I were to group the provisions listed above, I would do it like this:

PROGRAMMING FOR ALL CHILDREN	DIFFERENTIATION ACCORDING TO NEEDS OF CHILDREN WITH SPECIAL ABILITIES
• Teaching thinking skills • Having a science fair • Using Bloom's taxonomy	Workshops with artists

Activities which provide opportunities for all children may also allow special abilities to be used (such as an in-depth investigation for the science fair). However, they aren't set up specifically to cater for identified abilities.

Using this tool you might be able to see that you are doing quite a lot already in your school, both directly and indirectly, to provide for children with special abilities.

A further step is to analyse your practices more specifically. The questionnaire and supporting information on the next pages can guide you in this. It also helps you to answer the second question, "What else do we need to do?" by showing where the gaps are and leading you to think about what further action to take.

CWSA: WHERE ARE WE NOW AS A SCHOOL?

	YES	TO SOME DEGREE	NO	ACTION TO TAKE
PHILOSOPHY Do we have a shared philosophy on cwsa and their needs?				
DEFINITION Is our concept of special ability inclusive of: ▶ a wide range of abilities ▶ all ethnic groups ▶ potential and performance?				
IDENTIFICATION Do we have a responsive environment which allows abilities to show? Is there a school-wide identification process in place? Are multiple methods of identification used? Are parents/caregivers/whanau included in the identification process? Do we identify underachievers? Have teachers received professional development on recognising cwsa? Does identification lead to programming options being explored?				

CWSA: WHERE ARE WE NOW AS A SCHOOL?

	YES	TO SOME DEGREE	NO	ACTION TO TAKE
PROGRAMMING				
Is programming for cwsa an integral part of our planning?				
Is there flexibility of organisation and approach to programming?				
Are enrichment programmes based on individual identified needs?				
Are there opportunities for interaction with other students who share similar interests and talents?				
Do we use community resources and mentors to extend learning in areas of identified talent and special interest?				
Have teachers received professional development on programming for cwsa?				
Does a teacher or group co-ordinate identification and programming?				
POLICY				
Is there a written policy on children with special needs which includes cwsa?				
Does the policy need reviewing?				
Is this sufficient to guide programming for cwsa?				
Is there a written policy on cwsa?				
Does the policy need reviewing?				
Is there a budget to implement policy?				

CHILDREN WITH SPECIAL ABILITIES: SCHOOL PRIORITIES FOR ACTION

WHAT	HOW	WHERE	WHO	WHEN

SECTION 2
What are we doing? What do we need to do?

gifted and talented children: a planning guide

THINKING IT THROUGH:
Using the Questionnaire

This part is appropriate for all teaching staff in your school. A teacher facilitator or someone with a particular interest or expertise in this field could guide this process.

PHILOSOPHY

Until there are some common understandings about who gifted children are and what their needs are, identification, programming and policy development will be hard to achieve effectively. Try setting up a situation where staff can discuss their ideas about giftedness. Here are four ideas for how this can be done.

1. At a staff meeting, seek teacher's reactions to statements such as these:

   ▶ Children can be gifted in only one area.
   ▶ It is elitist to cater for cwsa differently from other children.
   ▶ Gifted children will make it on their own.
   ▶ All children are gifted.
   ▶ We don't have any gifted children in our school.
   ▶ There are gifted children in all cultural and socio-economic groups.

   People will have differing ideas; that's fine, but they need to be aired and shared.

2. You may discuss whether children with special abilities also have special needs and if so, what they might be. It can be helpful for each person to think of a child they know, list their strengths, interests and qualities, how they behave, how others behave towards them, and what problems they have. Based on this information, what are these children's needs?

3. Extracts like those on page 10, which suggest a strong rationale for providing appropriately for gifted students, could be discussed at a staff meeting.

4. Discussing the animal school fable at the beginning of this section might lead to questions like:

   ▶ Do we wish to focus on deficits or strengths?
   ▶ Do we want to round out and hold back or break ceilings and strive for excellence?

Try setting up a situation where staff can discuss their ideas about giftedness.

SECTION 2
What are we doing? What do we need to do?

gifted and talented children: a planning guide

- *The development of giftedness is the result of an interactive process that involves challenges from the environment that stimulate and bring forth innate talents, capabilities, and processes ... We either progress or regress intellectually; stability or maintenance of a fixed quantity of intelligence is not possible. Giftedness, as a label for a high level of intelligence, is a dynamic quality that can be furthered only by participation in learning experiences that challenge and extend from the point of the child's talent, ability and interest. (Clark, 1997, p6-7)*

- *Equality of educational opportunity does not mean "the same for all" or "uniformity of treatment". Rather it means that all students, including those with special abilities, have an equal right to educational programmes that will assist them to achieve to their highest potential. (Education Review Office, 1998, p7)*

DEFINITIONS

Giftedness

There is no one definition of **giftedness** nor general agreement about terminology. If you have a shared understanding in your school about abilities and needs you can decide on the terminology with which you feel most comfortable — gifted, gifted behaviour, talented, special ability, high ability and so on.

The concept of giftedness varies from culture to culture and over time. Each school might look at the cultural groups that make up their community and aim to make sure that its understandings about giftedness take account of relevant cultural values.

The concept of giftedness varies from culture to culture and over time.

For example, Bevan Brown (1996) says that concepts of special abilities for Māori should be viewed as holistic in nature, reflecting Māori values, customs and beliefs. In research, she found that Māori value a wide range of abilities and qualities including spiritual, cognitive, affective, aesthetic, linguistic, artistic, musical, psychomotor, social, intuitive, creative and leadership.

SECTION 2
What are we doing? What do we need to do?

gifted and talented children: a planning guide

A definition should be underpinned by understandings about:

▸ a wide range of abilities

▸ abilities and qualities valued by the various ethnic groups which make up your school population

▸ potential for gifted behaviour as well as achievement or performance already manifested

▸ those who have disabilities or specific learning difficulties as well as special abilities.

Being inclusive in this way might mean you may identify 15% of your school population rather than only 1 - 2% as in the past. However, specifying actual numbers or percentages is not particularly helpful, as this will vary over time.

Creativity

There is no agreement, about **creativity** either – about whether it is a category of ability or a way of applying intelligence which results in gifted behaviour. Some definitions explain creativity as changing ways of doing things or ways of thinking, first having mastered the traditional way. Others say it also incorporates complexity of personality; in particular being able to operate at both ends of many polarities like fantasy and reality, physical energy and rest or quiet, convergent and divergent thinking, concentrated attention and playful curiosity, sociability and need for solitude. In children and adolescents creativity is likely to be marked by intense curiosity, unusual interests, innovating or tinkering and a feeling of marginality rather than popularity.

The important point to bear in mind is that creativity must be a valued part of how special abilities are defined.

Multiple Intelligences

A high level of potential in any of the **multiple intelligences** as outlined by Howard Gardner (1983) can also be incorporated into a concept of special abilities. His theory suggests that individual strengths should be identified as well as strengths relative to the wider population (Ramos-Ford & Gardner, 1997). Based on this idea, a child might have a particular ability in mathematics in comparison to other curriculum areas. This "mathematical strength" might see her operating at about one year above average. Another child may have mathematical ability several years in advance of most of her age peers. The former has a *relative strength* in maths; the latter has a *potential giftedness* in maths. Identification of multiple intelligences will be discussed further in Section 3: Getting into School-wide Action.

IDENTIFICATION AND PROGRAMMING

Two Sides of the Same Coin

Identification and programming are linked and are both continuous processes. Learning activities provided in a responsive environment for all children lead to abilities surfacing and having an outlet, allowing teachers to notice that these talents exist. Flexible programming can respond to needs based on the abilities.

RESPONSIVE ENVIRONMENT (SCHOOL AND CLASS)

↓

allows

SPECIAL ABILITIES TO BECOME APPARENT

↓

which helps to

IDENTIFY NEEDS

↓

which leads to

APPROPRIATE PROGRAMMING OPTIONS

↓

which are part of the

RESPONSIVE ENVIRONMENT

Identifying an able child sounds easy and sometimes it is, if they perform at a high level at school, are articulate, outgoing and motivated. But what if an able child is not motivated at school, is underachieving, has a learning style inconsistent with the general style of the classroom, speaks a first language which is different from that of the teaching language of the classroom or has a disability? We may not detect this child so easily. Even some of the children profiled at the beginning of the book might not be identified by their teachers as having special abilities. John, Tom, Greta, William and Michelle may be underachieving, hiding their abilities or have the kind of abilities that are not so easily recognised or valued.

SECTION 2
What are we doing? What do we need to do?

gifted and talented children: a planning guide

"Do we identify children's abilities and then plan to meet those needs or do we set up 'programmes' and then decide who to put in them?"

The key to identifying these children lies in providing an environment which is *responsive* to their needs. A responsive environment is one which is supportive of diversity and individual differences, where relationships are co-operative and respectful and that is emotionally safe and cognitively stimulating. In an environment characterised by trust and acceptance, children's talents are likely to flourish and be noticed.

The significance of a responsive environment to the identification process is three-fold:

▸ It shows all children that they are valued, that differences are OK and therefore they can be themselves. In this environment they won't have to hide behind withdrawal and bad behaviour and teachers will see their talents.

▸ Teaching styles reflect variety and so teachers get an opportunity to observe how children respond when given choice or presented with different approaches.

▸ The input of parents or caregivers is encouraged, so the school receives the most valuable identification possible as parents know their children best.

It is important that identification does not become an end in itself. Children's names are sometimes entered on lists and registers, but not much else happens. This is at best pointless and at worst labelling for labelling's sake.

Providing specific programmes without identifying what abilities and needs learners have is equally pointless. This leads to piecemeal provisions, not necessarily linked to the needs of the children. Schools could ask themselves this question.

"Do we identify children's abilities and then plan to meet those needs or do we set up 'programmes' and then decide who to put in them?"

A scenario that looks at a piecemeal provision is described next.

THE PIECEMEAL APPROACH

School X decides to provide some enrichment programmes. Members of staff recognise that they have able children and some parents are putting on the pressure. So they decide to provide maths enrichment in Term 2 for Years 5 - 6 because Mrs Y is keen to teach maths. Teachers then look for children to put in the group. In Term 3 they will have creative writing for Years 3 - 4 for one hour a week, to give a different age group a turn. Term 4 is a bit busy to have enrichment as an extra.

WHAT'S GOOD AND BAD ABOUT THIS APPROACH?

▸ It recognises that able children have needs **BUT** doesn't establish what they are.

▸ It demonstrates good intentions **BUT** is it known that maths and writing are the priorities at those year levels?

▸ It shows that the school is listening and responding to parents **BUT** only to those applying pressure.

▸ It uses teacher strengths and interests **BUT** it needs to also base programming on children's needs.

▸ It provides some enrichment **BUT** sees it as an "extra" rather than an integral part of programming.

... having someone to co-ordinate identification and programming along with developing a policy would help to guide the process ...

What happens to students included in those enrichmnent groups at the end of the term's special programme? Are they left deflated? Perhaps there are Year 2 artists or Year 4 scientists languishing unchallenged in classrooms. Are their needs being met?

Perhaps, then, having someone to co-ordinate identification and programming along with developing a policy would help to guide the process so that good intentions are turned into good practice rather than into ad hoc, short-term provisions.

Ideas outlined in later sections of this book show how to link identification with programming.

Policy

Some schools have a policy on children with special needs which includes children with special abilities. This can be supported with a Procedures booklet or an Action Plan in relation to children with special abilities. Other schools have found that children with special abilities get overlooked in such a broad policy and prefer to develop a separate policy for those with special abilities. This is an individual school decision.

SECTION 2
What are we doing? What do we need to do?

gifted and talented children: a planning guide

Before you begin work on your policy rationale, begin with a philosophical debate as suggested on page 6. This debate needs to be set in the context of reality, for example the requirements of national and state frameworks which outline what *has* to be done. Both philosophy and mandatory requirements will help you to come up with your rationale.

A policy is an evolving document. Regard it as tentative and come back to it. Decide how it fits with other policies.

So the "why" of providing for children with special abilities is a matter of asking:

▸ What do we believe?

▸ What are we required to do?

▸ How do we integrate the two?

A POSSIBLE WAY FOR DEVELOPING A POLICY

RATIONALE	Why we do need to cater appropriately for children with special abilities?
GOALS (PURPOSES)	What do we want to achieve in our school for these children in the long term?
GUIDELINES	
Definition	Who are children with special abilities in our school population?
Identification	How do we identify a range of abilities?
Programming	What are our programming options in the classroom and school?
Evaluation	How do we assess and evaluate individual progress and overall programming?
IMPLEMENTATION	
Staff development	What is needed?
Liaison with parents	How to achieve?
Budget/resources	Amount allocated, from what source, for what purposes?
Co-ordination	Person/ group of people to co-ordinate for school.

CREATIVE PROBLEM-SOLVING

There are common barriers to achieving what we want in schools. Having had philosophical discussions and having devised a policy as a staff, some of you are raring to go but there still may be roadblocks. This is to be expected whenever new ideas or changes are being introduced.

This Creative Problem-Solving activity, in six steps, is one way to make the process of addressing the barriers more manageable.

STEP 1

Discuss general problem areas associated with providing for children with special abilities.

- staff attitudes.
- funding / resourcing
- difficulty of identification
- parental expectations
- expertise of staff
- time factors.

STEP 2

Decide on **one** main problem to address as a staff.

STEP 3

Articulate all that is known about the problem

For example, who is involved, who it affects.

STEP 4

Brainstorm possible solutions.

Accept them all at this stage.

Write the potential solutions onto a Rating Sheet.

STEP 5

Decide on criteria by which to judge the ideas.

Rate each idea on a 1 to 5 scale.

Add up the scores to find the best solution.

STEP 6

Write a plan for putting the solution into action.

SECTION 2
What are we doing? What do we need to do?

gifted and talented children: a planning guide

So far in this planning guide you've:

▸ looked at what you are doing already

▸ identified what needs to be done

▸ talked philosophy

▸ come up with a definition

▸ maybe begun to draft or review policy

▸ identified barriers.

The next two sections outline the "How to..." How can we identify abilities and needs, and programme accordingly? Section 3 looks at school-wide action and Section 4 provides classroom strategies.

SECTION 3
GETTING INTO SCHOOL-WIDE ACTION: HOW DO WE DO IT?

IDENTIFICATION IN THE SCHOOL AND CLASSROOM

When you create a responsive environment, children's abilities have an opportunity to surface and be noticed. Teachers need to give children chances to show their abilities independently, in a group and also when "scaffolded" by adults. Families and others outside of the school can contribute valuable information about children's strengths, achievements and interests. Using a combination of the methods listed below will increase the likelihood that abilities will be noticed.

WHO	HOW
TEACHERS	▸ create a responsive environment
	▸ observe using checklists or rating scales of characteristics
	▸ observe and record anecdotally
	▸ use tests – standardised achievement, intelligence, classroom
	▸ evaluate products / examples of work / performances – group and individual
	▸ take note of competition results
PARENTS/ COMMUNITY	▸ being involved in school/ home conferences
	▸ responding to questionnaires
	▸ filling in rating scales of characteristics
	▸ providing anecdotal information
	▸ showing examples of children's products
STUDENTS	▸ filling in interest/ strength inventories
	▸ self-nominating for programmes
	▸ achieving awards outside of school

On the following page is a case study of Judy and how her school environment has responded to her particular needs.

JUDY: A CASE STUDY

9 year old Judy's abilities have been identified in a variety of ways at her school. It has been noticed that she shows:

▸ **many of the indicators of general ability**

identified by her class teacher using a checklist of characteristics of general ability.

▸ **a high level of interpersonal and intrapersonal intelligences**

identified by teacher observation and parent information. For example, Judy cares deeply about issues; is reflective, has empathy.

▸ **specific abilities in oral language, reading, written language and research/ investigation**

identified by very high PAT language scores; publication of stories in the School Journal and letters to the editor; self-nomination for the debating club.

▸ **many characteristics of creativity**

identified by teacher and parent observation of such things as: originality in written work, challenge of the status quo in regard to environmental issues; enjoyment of periods of solitude.

▸ **a high level of task commitment**

identified by teacher observation and parent report of Judy's self motivation in investigating real issues, writing, debating.

On the next page is an example of an identification process that your school can use. This approach helps providing for children with special abilities to be a collaborative process and a collective responsibility. Each teacher fills in the identification form using information from a variety of sources. Teachers then meet to decide on programming options together.

It can be used a few weeks into the school year when you have begun to get to know the children in your class but wish to know them better. However, the process is continuous and entries can be made throughout the year. Collated information should be carried forward and used next year for ongoing programming. The identification process does not stop here as abilities surface at different times and can be perceived differently by individual teachers.

IDENTIFICATION FORM: CHILDREN WITH SPECIAL ABILITIES

TIME PERIOD FOR COMPLETION OF FORM: _____

Further names can be added throughout the year. Date entries.

ABOVE AVERAGE ABILITY	NOMINATIONS	TEACHER	OTHER SOURCES
A. GENERAL ABILITY INDICATORS If students show quite a number of these characteristics, record their names. • displays logical and analytical thinking • is quick to see patterns and relationships • is able to understand complex concepts and abstraction • achieves quick mastery of information • easily grasps underlying principles • likes intellectual challenge • jumps stages in learning • problem-finds as well as problem-solves • reasons things out for self • formulates and supports ideas with evidence • can recall a wide range of knowledge • independently seeks to discover the why and how of things • is concerned about moral and ethical issues; strong sense of justice • has a high level of sensitivity and empathy			

ABOVE AVERAGE ABILITY	NOMINATIONS	TEACHER	OTHER SOURCES

B. GENERAL ABILITY – MULTIPLE INTELLIGENCES

If a student demonstrates a high level of any one intelligence, record their name.

- Bodily-kinesthetic — physical movement and knowledge of use of the body
- Interpersonal — relationships and communication; understanding others
- Intrapersonal — knowledge of own thinking and emotions
- Linguistic — use of words and language
- Logical-mathematical — mathematic and scientific reasoning
- Musical — sensitivity to rhythm, tonal patterns; performance and composition
- Naturalist — curiosity about natural world; ability to classify flora and fauna
- Spatial — comprehension of the visual world; creation of mental images

C. SPECIFIC ABILITIES

This means characteristics of general above average ability (as outlined in Section A) are applied to a specialised area of knowledge or performance. Write names beside each specific area.

Sometimes it may be a group of students collectively who show ability.

- Culturally valued abilities / qualities _____
- Oral language _____
- Reading _____
- Written language _____
- Drama _____
- Languages other than English _____
- Māori language _____
- Other language _____
- Mathematics _____
- Science _____
- Technology _____
- Construction/mechanical _____
- Information technology _____
- Physical education _____
- Health _____
- Sport _____
- Art _____
- Craft _____
- Dance _____
- Music _____
- Social studies _____
- Research/investigation _____
- Leadership _____
- Other _____

ABOVE AVERAGE ABILITY	NOMINATIONS	TEACHER	OTHER SOURCES
D. UNDERACHIEVERS List students whom you feel *may* have special abilities, but are underachieving. They may demonstrate some of the following: • being disruptive, day dreaming, manipulating • self criticism • having a subtle sense of humour, a strong sense of justice • determination, strong interests outside of school • difficulty with writing • asking lots of questions • rarely completing work • learning in a spatial rather than a sequential style Also include here children whose main spoken language is not the same as the language of instruction in the classroom (if you feel they may have abilities as yet unseen).			

FOR CLASSROOM USE

a. Refer to these lists when planning learning activities and incorporate appropriate challenge for these students.

b. Put a ring around names if you feel that differentiation other than in the classroom is needed. (This may be to cater for the type of interest / level of ability / degree of creativity or to break a pattern of underachievement or give the chance for task commitment to develop.)

c. Look for evidence of creativity and task commitment being applied to the ability areas. (Refer to indicators following)

d. Observe closely those students listed as underachievers. More data may need to be gathered.

FOR SCHOOL USE

a. Enter on a school or syndicate/department list the names of those students who need differentiation other than in the regular class programme (from b above).

b. Decide collectively how to programme for the needs of these students.

c. Review this on a regular basis.

d. Personal profile sheets can be useful to record information .

CREATIVITY INDICATORS

▸ fluency of ideas but also ability to select what is significant

▸ flexibility and originality of thought

▸ willingness to challenge the existing way of doing things

▸ openness to that which is new and different

▸ intensely curious, speculative

▸ adventurous, willing to take risks

▸ sensitive to detail; aesthetic qualities

▸ unusual interests

▸ ability to tolerate solitude

▸ keen sense of humour

▸ complexity of personality

TASK COMMITMENT INDICATORS

▸ high level of interest, enthusiasm, fascination and involvement in problem or chosen area of study

▸ intrinsic motivation; work because love to, not have to

▸ perseverance, endurance, determination, hard work, dedicated practice

▸ self confidence in ability to achieve

▸ setting high standards for one's work

ABOUT THE IDENTIFICATION FORM

The indicators on this form have been compiled from a wide variety of sources including McAlpine & Reid (1996), Ramos-Ford & Gardner (1997) and Renzulli & Reis (1985).

If you use a multiple intelligences approach to assessment of individual needs and programming in your school, it is worthwhile to link this to the process of identifying special abilities. This approach may increase the likelihood of noticing intrapersonal, interpersonal and spatial intelligences which are sometimes undervalued.

Interpersonal and intrapersonal intelligences can also collectively be called emotional intelligence. This includes self awareness of feelings, strengths and weaknesses, managing moods, being motivated towards goals, having empathy and being able to persuade or lead others (Goleman,1996). It is important in a responsive environment to recognise this kind of intelligence along with specific academic abilities. Emotional giftedness may entail having these attributes to a high degree but also a strong sense of justice, acute sensitivity to moral and ethical issues and intensity of feeling. This can sometimes mean acting against adult authority if it is seen as unjust (Piechowski, 1997).

Spatial intelligence may sometimes link to underachievement as this style of learning can be incompatible with the sequential learning emphasised in school. Spatial learners see the big picture without having to go through all the steps. They do well on tasks involving abstract concepts, visualisation, solving puzzles and problems, designing, constructing and mind mapping but may be poor at rote learning, phonics, spelling and computation. It is therefore, necessary to identify this as a particular kind of ability, rather than as a deficit.

> See p61 for further reading on emotional intelligence and emotional giftedness, identification of multiple intelligences, spatial learners and underachievement.

IDENTIFICATION OF ABILITIES AND NEEDS

If you have identified special abilities in children, then you will be able to determine their learning needs.

Let's return to the earlier example of Judy who showed:

▸ most of the indicators of general ability

▸ a high level of linguistic, interpersonal and intrapersonal intelligence

▸ specific abilities in oral language, reading, written language and research/investigation

▸ many of the characteristics of creativity

▸ a high level of task commitment.

Her learning needs may be:

▸ to compact the time spent on "the basics"

▸ to have the opportunity to study topics in depth

▸ to have the opportunity to self select topics

▸ to have the opportunity to work on real issues with others who feel strongly about them

▸ to have the opportunity to interact orally with others

▸ to have the opportunity to self assess.

From the following case study, list Sam's characteristics / type of abilities then work out what his learning needs might be.

SAM: A CASE STUDY

Sam is 7 years 2 months of age, in Year 3. In school he is particularly interested in and also good at maths problem–solving, drawing, constructing and talking. He sometimes makes jokes that only the teacher understands. He comes up with a lot of ideas when the class or a group are involved in problem solving. He cannot always explain his maths reasoning but appears to make mental leaps and finds unusual ways to solve problems. He often gets computation wrong. He has messy printing, does not like writing stories, and can read reasonably well but does not do so by choice.

He gets on well with other children and with adults.

Out of school he also loves talking (and arguing), having intelligent conversations with adults. He spends hours making elaborate constructions mainly out of Lego and loves to know how things work. He plays chess and board games with anyone who will play, sometimes beating his parents.

SAM'S CHARACTERISTICS / ABILITIES: ....

....

....

....

SAM'S LEARNING NEEDS: ....

....

....

....

We will come back to Sam shortly.

LEARNING NEEDS AND PROGRAMMING OPTIONS

After learning needs are established, programming options to meet those needs are easier to plan. Sometimes there is only one child in a class operating at a particular level or with a specific interest. This is when the wider school and community environments can be explored for programming options.

WHAT ARE SOME OF THE OPTIONS TO CHOOSE FROM?

▸ **Differentiation in the classroom** – adapting to suit the abilities of the individual:

- content (the ideas, concepts, information taught and learnt)
- process (the way in which content is presented and activities through which students learn)
- products (demonstration of learning).

▸ **Whole school enrichment** – enrichment for all children in mixed ability or like ability groups for a block of time e.g. half day a week.

▸ **Independent learning room** – to work together on a project such as producing a newspaper or in a room set up with challenging learning centres.

▸ **Mentorships** – older student, workforce member, parent, retired person or any teacher to work with the child in shared area of interest. Also consider e-mail mentorships.

▸ **Buddies** – two children together to work in area of interest.

▸ **Cross-age enrichment groups** – in areas of curriculum, cross-curricula investigations, leadership, oral language, dramatic performance, community projects.

▸ **Workshops** – a block of time e.g. with an author or artist.

▸ **Inter-school programmes** – several primary schools offer different subjects or programmes offered at intermediates for primary children.

HOW CAN THESE OPTIONS BE IMPLEMENTED?

▸ Establish an inventory of child / teacher / community expertise.

▸ IEPs to set goals (translated from needs) and detail provisions to be made.

▸ Basing programmes on established models e.g. Enrichment Triad (Renzulli)* see below.

▸ Teacher facilitator to set up individual investigations or mentorships.

▸ Permanent clustering of several able children in one classroom.

▸ Ability grouping in classroom or between classes.

▸ Curriculum compacting i.e. spending less time on the "basics" to allow for independent work of choice or accelerated content.

▸ Acceleration of class level.

▸ Regrouping of classes for certain time periods, clustering able children together.

*ENRICHMENT TRIAD MODEL

This model involves three types of interlinking enrichment. Type I and II activities are suitable for all children, although they may be introduced at varying levels or differing pace. Type III is more suited to children with special abilities.

Type I   General Exploratory Activities

to acquaint the children with a variety of topics and interest areas. Some of these may lead to a Type III independent project.

Type II   Group Training Activities

to develop cognitive and affective processes e.g: research and problem–solving skills, values, self awareness.

Type III   Individual and Small Group Investigations

to investigate real problems or produce original performances or products for real audiences.

(Renzulli, 1977; Renzulli & Reis, 1991 in Davis & Rimm, 1994)

IDENTIFYING A CO-ORDINATOR

If you undertake a school-wide approach to identification and programming, it is useful to have a teacher or teachers co-ordinating the process. Co-ordinators could:

▶ meet with the leaders of teams or syndicates regarding the list of identified children who need differentiation within the wider school context, to consider programming options

▶ help identify staff development needs

▶ provide information to staff about identification and resources available.

What about Programming Options for Judy?

Many of Judy's needs can be provided for in the classroom through strategies like those suggested in the next section of this planning guide. However, opportunities may also be sought for her to have oral language enrichment with others of high ability and time to work on real issues in the school or community. A mentor for her writing would be valuable.

And Sam?

Most of Sam's needs can also be provided for in the classroom. Within the wider school context, oral and art enrichment opportunities and extracurricula time or electives for board games and chess may be possible. Information about Sam's characteristics, abilities, needs and suggested programming for him is summarised on an Individual Profile form (see next page).

A sheet like this is not necessary for every child who has a special ability but may be useful for the following purposes:

▶ for an exceptionally able child who needs a variety of learning environments

▶ to particularly focus on strengths and interests for an underachieving child or one who has unusual learning styles

▶ when parents are unhappy about a school's provisions and detailed information needs to be gathered and discussed.

INDIVIDUAL PROFILE FOR ___ *Sam*

GENERAL CHARACTERISTICS	MULTIPLE INTELLIGENCES	SPECIFIC ABILITIES	STRONG INTERESTS	INDICATORS OF CREATIVITY	EVIDENCE OF TASK COMMITMENT
quick to see patterns	linguistic (oral)	chess	chess	fluency of ideas	chooses to construct, draw, play chess at home and school and concentrates for a long time on them
understands complex concepts	logical/mathematical	oral language	board games	flexibility	
quick mastery of information	spatial	maths problem–solving	building Lego models	challenges existing way of doing things	
grasps underlying principles		drawing	drawing	openness to new and different ideas	
likes intellectual challenge			talking	curious	
jumps stages in learning				adventurous, risk taking	
problem–finds and problem–solves				sensitive to detail, aesthetics	
reasons things out for self				keen sense of humour	
seeks to discover how and why of things					

INDIVIDUAL PROFILE FOR _Sam_

MEANS OF IDENTIFICATION: Teacher observation – general characteristics (from school-wide identification sheet), specific abilities. Self nomination for chess club. Parent information – interests, abilities, task commitment.

LEARNING NEEDS: Opportunities to respond to tasks in own style i.e. oral, visual–spatial, hands–on; not just sequential or written. Opportunities for engagement with other children with like abilities – oral, artistic, chess, problem–solving. Opportunities to extend skills in areas of ability.

SUGGESTED PROVISIONS

WHAT	WHEN/WHERE
Oral discussion, problem solving, debate	Classroom language groups
	Cross age Year 3–5 Oral enrichment group Term 2
Drawing skills & techniques	Cross-age Workshop with parent/artist: half day for 6 weeks
	Using techniques from workshop in classroom
Choice of style of product for work	Classroom tasks/ projects/independent studies
Play chess & board games	Friday afternoon electives with others who choose to do so
	Monday lunchtime club

RECORD OF PROVISIONS

▶ EVALUATION

To assess the appropriateness of programmes, ask yourself the following questions before you undertake them. Also do this during the programme and at the end.

▸ Will all children be interested in the content?

▸ Could all children participate successfully?

If the answers are "yes", then *all* children should be involved. Differentiation based on learning needs of children with special abilities has not occurred.

"Yes" should be the answer to these next questions:

▸ Does the programme differentiate any or all of the following: content, process, product, learning environment to suit individual needs?

▸ Are any or all of the following being further developed: abilities, skills, self esteem, perseverance, creativity?

Some of the following assessment methods could be used in answering the last two questions:

▸ Student self-assessment through oral discussion, conferencing, questionnaires or reflective diaries.

▸ Product evaluation forms with specific criteria.

▸ 'Expert' evaluation of product or performance e.g. by an artist, high school teacher.

▸ Pre- and post- tests.

▸ Parent questionnaires asking about their perception of child's progress in and reaction to programme.

▸ Individual portfolios which document progress over time.

Other aspects which might be evaluated are:

Time frames – were they long enough to achieve goals and to really extend abilities?

Suitability of those running programmes – have they had professional development? Do they have the necessary conceptual knowledge?

Involvement of parents and community – in teaching, mentoring, providing advice, facilitating visits.

AN EXAMPLE OF GETTING INTO SCHOOL–WIDE ACTION

PRIMARY SCHOOL
ROLL: 200 STUDENTS, ORGANISED INTO 3 SYNDICATES

DURING MARCH

Each classroom teacher filled out an identification form (see pp. 20-23 of this guide). In addition to teacher observation, testing and parent / caregiver input, a Problem–Solving week was held school-wide with teachers and outside consultants running workshops, some with mixed age groups, on curriculum and cross-curriculum problem–solving, including outdoor pursuits. Teachers focused on observing children in different settings, getting insights into interests, creativity, oral language ability, leadership, ability to think at higher levels and problem–solve.

END MARCH

Syndicate leaders collated information.

EARLY APRIL

At each syndicate meeting, needs were discussed and some decisions made; for example, the middle syndicate decided on:

- ▶ the need for professional development on classroom strategies.

- ▶ some cross-class grouping occurred for science with a teacher who has strengths in teaching science to those with special abilities

- ▶ independent study was based on Renzulli's Enrichment Triad Model, teaching advanced Type II skills to facilitate the study and using parents to facilitate trips out of school for Type III investigations

- ▶ sending a form to parents seeking help for trips to facilitate independent study (syndicate leader to arrange this through designated co-ordinator).

MID APRIL

Syndicate leaders met with cwsa co-ordinator and principal and decided:

- ▶ that a teacher who had undertaken study on cwsa would facilitate a staff meeting on classroom strategies. Further needs would be determined at that meeting

- ▶ a form would be sent to all parents seeking help with trips

- ▶ to buddy a few children between syndicates to facilitate specific interests.

AUGUST

At syndicate meetings, teachers discussed progress and needs.

END TERM 3

Syndicate leaders met with cwsa co-ordinator to discuss evaluation of programmes, needs for Term 4 and possible resourcing needs for next year.

In the school in the above example, as in the majority of schools, children with special abilities will spend most of their time in the regular classroom with their age peers. Therefore, it is essential that all teachers know how to provide challenging programmes in their classrooms. The final section of this resource introduces some ideas on how to make learning meaningful for children with special abilities in the classroom.

SECTION 4
WHAT CAN WE DO IN THE CLASSROOM?

► PROVIDING A RESPONSIVE ENVIRONMENT

A responsive classroom environment will help to cater for special abilities. Responsive means a classroom that takes account of all students' physical, psychological and cognitive needs. Able children in particular often need a variety of physical settings and groupings to cater for their cognitive and affective needs. Flexible school-wide organisation and tolerance of high mobility will also allow these children to interact with a range of people of varying ages. The suggestions for creating a responsive environment which follow, however, make the assumption that most children will spend much of their time in regular classrooms. The suggestions look at what differentiation of content, process and product means within a safe environment for risk-taking and creativity. Strategies for cognitive development are outlined, followed by strategies for emotional development. The two, however, are intertwined as acknowledging cognitive needs and providing for them contributes to positive emotional development.

First take some time to reflect on the questions following. Nobody's perfect – if you answer "yes" to some of the questions, you're doing much to provide a responsive environment for children with special abilities already, but you might see something that you can work on.

Responsive means a classroom that takes account of all students' physical, psychological and cognitive needs.

DO I PROVIDE A RESPONSIVE ENVIRONMENT?

	YES	TO SOME DEGREE	NO	ACTION TO TAKE
Are cwsa in my class happy, fulfilled students who want to come to school?				
Do I keep an open mind when a parent says their child has a special ability or needs more challenge?				
Do I provide for a wide range of abilities in children from all ethnic groups?				
Do I focus more on strengths than weaknesses even if children are underachieving or have specific learning difficulties?				
Do I acknowledge that it is okay for cwsa to know more than me about some things?				
Do I allow for a variety of learning styles and multiple intelligences?				
Do I ensure that children are challenged to work toward their full potential rather than cruising along?				
Do I make sure children don't have to repeat and practise what they already know?				
Do I allow cwsa to learn at their own pace / rate?				
Do I allow for in–depth study of areas of interest?				
Do I allow personal goal–setting and encourage self evaluation?				
Do I encourage creativity, risk-taking and original responses?				
Do I encourage higher level thinking?				
Do I allow for flexibility of grouping including the choice of working alone?				
Do I cater for the social and emotional needs of cwsa?				

PERSONAL PRIORITY FOR ACTION: ....

LEARNING AND TEACHING STRATEGIES

In the classroom, you can provide for cognitive needs in all or some of the following ways which allow for differentiation of content, process and product.

CONTENT – what a child should know, understand and be able to do.
For children with special abilities this should include abstraction, complexity, advanced subject matter and cross-curricula subject matter.

PROCESS – the way in which children learn the content.
For children with special abilities this should include higher level thinking skills, discovery, choice, faster pace, depth.

PRODUCT – what children produce to demonstrate what they have learned.
For children with special abilities this includes choice of style of presentation, transformation of information and communication to an audience.

INDEPENDENT/SELF DIRECTED LEARNING

Some children with special abilities have unusual, advanced or what seem like obsessional interests. Allowing children to work independently can cater for several needs:

▸ to pursue an area of interest

▸ to really delve into something in depth (own choice or class unit)

▸ to pursue a "real" topic

▸ to work at own pace

▸ to use own creative ideas and devise creative products

▸ to increase perseverance, motivation, self esteem.

How can you find time for this in the class programme?

▸ In theme time, allow the more independent children to work with less direction from the teacher.

▸ Incorporate "givens" and choice into units.

▸ Base activities in a unit on Treffinger's model (see over).

▸ Compact time on the basics to build time for independent study.

INCORPORATING INDEPENDENCE
(BASED ON TREFFINGER'S SELF-DIRECTED LEARNING MODEL)

There are four levels of self-direction in this model so it is possible for all the class to be working on a topic with varying degrees of depth and independence. (Treffinger, 1975 in Maker & Neilson, 1995)

1. TEACHER-DIRECTED

At this level, those who need firm guidance will carry out activities set by the teacher. It may be that all children will do some of these activities at the beginning of a unit then the more independent will move to other steps.

2. SOME CHOICE WITHIN TEACHER-CREATED OPTIONS

The teacher still sets the activities but the children choose what they will do and in which order. The content can be the same for all or can be differentiated so that there are higher level activities for some children.

One way of doing this is to use **hopscotch contracts** (p.39). If the content is designed for different groups, each child must do each step but in their own time. If the content is the same for all, children with special abilities could miss out the first two steps (compacting) and do the rest of the steps. The steps could be based on Bloom's taxonomy.

If they can cope easily with this they can use a **noughts and crosses grid** (p.40) which allows a choice of three out of nine activities as well as the order in which they do them.

These simple contracts can be used in any subject area as well as cross curriculum. They can be based on content or could focus on practising skills such as taking notes, interviewing and approaches to work such as different styles of gathering information or styles of presenting work. They can also incorporate the multiple intelligences by including activities using the full range of intelligences.

The following hopscotch could be used by junior or middle primary children with special abilities, individually or with a partner. They need sound reading and thinking ability and a degree of independence.

They could:

- ▸ do each step
- ▸ do number 1 and three others
- ▸ do number 1, one from 2, 3, 4 and two from 5, 6, 7, 8

The hopscotch activities incorporate the use of communication skills, information skills, work and study skills. They are based on the different types of thinking in Bloom's taxonomy.

This hopscotch could also be used by all children with an interest in dinosaurs, if reading material at a suitable level is provided and if manageable steps are chosen.

HOPSCOTCH CONTRACT: DINOSAURS

AFFECTIVE

7. How do you feel about dinosaurs? (tape, draw, write)

8. Do you believe it was inevitable that dinosaurs would become extinct? Why? (write, debate)

EVALUATION

6. Create a dinosaur which could survive today. (draw, model, diagram)

SYNTHESIS

ANALYSIS

4. Compare the characteristics of the dinosaurs you have studied. (write, chart, table, Venn diagram)

5. Show which parts of the world dinosaurs lived in. (map, globe)

APPLICATION

3. Make a timeline of when dinosaurs lived. (pictures, words, model)

COMPREHENSION

2. What are five interesting facts you've found out? (tape, write, draw)

KNOWLEDGE

1. Find information and read about at least five species of dinosaur.

INFORMATION

3. TEACHER AND CHILD CREATE OPTIONS TOGETHER

Once children have the skills to manage choice and their own time, allow for more open-ended activities and more input to the learning activities from them. Continue to teach further independent learning skills such as devising a good open-ended question. Create activities together or specify non-negotiables and allow them to devise the rest of the activities. Children can create noughts and crosses menus based on their interests or have some free choice squares in a teacher–made grid. Negotiate timeframes. Encourage some self and peer evaluation.

The following noughts and crosses grid would be suitable for middle or upper primary students and can provide an opportunity for children with special abilities interested in leadership to explore issues in depth and also become involved in leadership. Children could choose to work individually or in a pair or group of three.

It fits in with the Social Organisation / Community and Participation strand of the Social Studies / SOSE curriculum.

NOUGHTS AND CROSSES CONTRACT WITH LEADERSHIP AS THE KEY CONCEPT

Make a study of the reasons why people become leaders. Give examples of individuals who have become leaders in each of these ways.	What style of leader would you like to be? Why?	Write several generalisations (i.e. statements that you believe always apply) about leadership.
Plan a leadership initiative in which you could be involved in your school. Try to "sell" the idea to your teacher.	**FREE CHOICE**	Choose a great leader to study. Set yourself an open-ended question to find out about that person.
Design a concept map with leadership as the central concept.	What are the qualities of a good leader? Rank them in order of importance and justify your ranking.	Define and explore an issue of gender / culture / race and leadership.

Choose a line of three to do.

4. STUDENT–DIRECTED

Children set their own questions, carry out the independent learning, self-evaluate and present the results but still always negotiate this with the teacher.

A **goalpost contract** can be used. (This technique could initially be learned as a group). The steps are:

▸ On a large piece of card, write your question.

▸ Draw goalpost of favourite sport.

▸ Cut out balls for that sport and number them.

▸ Write each step in order on separate balls.

▸ Blu Tak balls on chart.

▸ Put each ball through/over goal as step is achieved.

A diary can be helpful for child-teacher communication so the teacher can see what help is requested on reading the diary after school.

An example of an investigation which a child with special abilities in the junior school could carry out is:

QUESTION: Were toys the same in the past as they are today?

STEPS:

1. Make up questions to ask children to find out what toys they play with.

2. Make up questions to ask adults to find out what toys they used to play with.

3. Ask questions of 10 teachers, parents or grandparents - record on tape.

4. Ask questions of 10 children - record on tape.

5. Draw a graph to show toys today / past.

6. Tell the other children about similarities/differences and show the graph.

Treffinger's model of self-direction can be used in conjunction with the Enrichment Triad Model outlined on p.29. Type II Renzulli skill learning fits with steps 2 and 3 of Treffinger's model. Treffinger's student self-directed learning step can be incorporated with Renzulli's ideas for Type III investigative work.

Allowing for increasing degrees of self-direction differentiates the process of learning and the content can be higher level or self selected. A range of products can also result.

Original products or performances can represent a synthesis of information the child finds into a new form. (Note that "original" means original for that child at that time, not new to the world! However, s/he may go on in adulthood to be a real creator i.e. a transformer of knowledge in a domain.)

Products may include:

- letter
- newsletter item
- song
- music
- "how to" book
- role play
- story for publication
- dance
- advertisement
- oral presentation
- map
- model
- OHT
- timeline
- computer-generated table
- painting
- graph
- demonstration.

Audiences for these products/performances may include:

- teacher
- children in class
- elderly people
- a child buddy
- mentor
- community group
- older children
- readers of school newsletter
- an e-mail pal
- parents.

Discovery Learning

Do children in your class sometimes say they are bored? Well, encourage them to **THINK**. Don't tell – let them discover. For example try teaching an alternative to regular multiplication. This could be to a group of children who have mastered long multiplication easily; they need a new challenge. The "telling" way would be to show them an example on the board and tell them how ancient Egyptian multiplication works. The "discovery" way works like this: Write up two examples on the board:

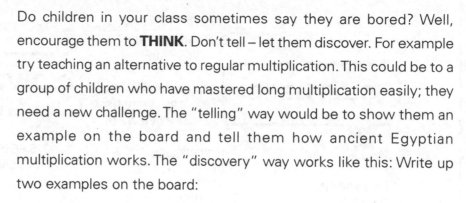

~~25 x 26~~	20 x 13
50 x 13	~~40 x 6~~
~~100 x 6~~	80 x 3
200 x 3	160 x 1
400 x 1	
650	260

Ask them to figure out how the system works. They will need to try more examples of their own to see if their theory works. (Can **you** see how the system works? See p.60 for an explanation!)

They can then investigate related questions such as why remainders are not used, why some examples take more steps than others, what happens when bigger numbers are used. Children end up doing lots of computation without being asked to!

Conceptual Learning

Concept maps, in which students diagrammatically represent relationships between concepts, can be used at the culmination of a unit of work to draw understandings together, or sometimes at the beginning to ascertain prior knowledge.

The key concept of the topic is written in the middle of a large piece of paper and related concepts are identified by either the teacher or the children. A good way to do this is to write each concept on a small piece of paper. They are then arranged on the large page with arrows drawn between them and joining words and phrases written in. Much discussion ensues as to where the concepts should go and how they relate. That is why having them on small pieces of paper is helpful so that they can be physically moved around.

CONCEPT MAP WITH BEAUTY AS THE CENTRAL CONCEPT

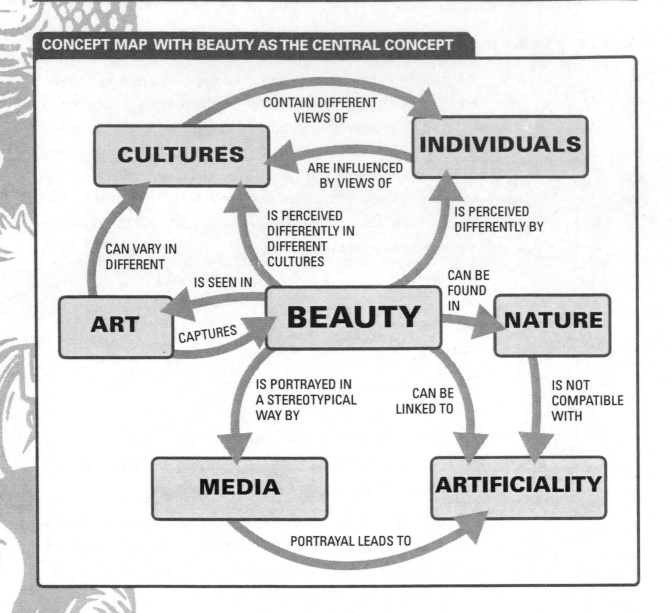

Concepts being studied by the class could be extended to draw out generalisations for investigation. For example, *patterns* help to predict what might happen; *heroes* differ in different cultures and in different eras; *discovery* leads to change; *cooperation* often requires compromise – compromise can be negative or positive.

Concepts which are of interest to able children in an ethical sense, in a cultural sense or because of their interest in world affairs can be studied and discussed. For example, the ethics of new technology, prejudice, conservation, extinction, diversity, stereotyping, animal rights and so on. How global issues are manifested locally might be explored, which could lead to questions like – what can we do as individuals? This approach could help to change a child's feeling of powerlessness to one of believing they can do something to make a difference.

SPECIFIC EXAMPLES OF PROVISIONS IN THE CLASSROOM

Let's return to the two case studies of Judy and Sam. Possibilities for provisions in the wider school have already been outlined.

School–wide

For example, for **Judy** suggestions were oral language enrichment, working on real issues in the school or community, a mentor for writing, being in the debating club.

In the classroom, where Judy will be much of the time, needs must also be met. There is a link between school and classroom programmes because strategies such as spending less time on practising the basics allows time for the wider school experiences.

What can be done for Judy in the classroom if her needs are:

▸ to compact the time spent on "the basics"?

▸ to study topics in depth?

▸ to self - select topics?

▸ to work on real issues with others who feel strongly about them?

▸ to interact orally with others?

▸ to self assess?

a. In most subjects, especially reading and written language instruction, Judy will not **always** need to be part of the group or do written practice exercises.

b. To study topics in depth, she will thrive on conceptual type learning and combining concepts into generalisations. This may be extension work within class units.

c. Self-selected topics could be pursued using compacted writing and reading time. Renzulli Type III investigative work with real outlets could be carried out alone or with a partner.

d. Studying real issues and coming up with some solutions may occur partly in and partly out of the classroom. She may work with someone from another class at times. Email links could also be established with other students who are interested in similar issues. Creative Problem–Solving about real issues could occur in class language group as well as in oral enrichment time.

e. In the classroom Judy will need some time in a like-ability group for oral language stimulation. The whole class could also have discussions in pairs, with the teacher allowing for pairs to be of like ability at times.

f. Setting goals and criteria for assessment as recommended by Treffinger and Renzulli will allow for input into her own learning as well as some responsibility for the outcomes.

School–wide

For **Sam**, suggestions in the wider school context were: oral and art enrichment opportunities, time for board games and chess.

His learning needs were identified as being:

▸ the need to respond to tasks in his own style i.e. oral, visual-spatial, hands-on, not just sequential or written

▸ the need for engagement with other children with like abilities – oral, artistic, chess, problem–solving

▸ the need to extend skills in areas of ability.

In the classroom programme, those needs could be provided for in these ways:

a. If the teacher is aware of multiple intelligences, children could be given the opportunity to respond to some tasks in a variety of ways like drawing a diagram, taping the answer, making a model. Noughts and crosses grids could incorporate choice of multiple intelligences activities. Sam should be allowed to get the answer in his own way in subjects like maths where he may not follow the usual steps.

b. Groups should be of likeability sometimes so that he can interact orally and in solving problems.

c. As Sam is good at art, construction, oral language, and maths problem solving and has many general characteristics of giftedness, he needs a chance to develop these abilities in the class programme. He would enjoy discussion around conceptual themes; being able to discover patterns and investigate in maths rather than being told and then made to practise; a chance for hands-on activities, not always written work; and an art project may be a self-selected area of study.

INDIVIDUAL PROFILE FOR

GENERAL CHARACTERISTICS (HIGHLIGHT CHARACTERISTICS WHICH APPLY)	MULTIPLE INTELLIGENCES (HIGHLIGHT IDENTIFIED INTELLIGENCES)	SPECIFIC ABILITIES	STRONG INTERESTS	INDICATORS OF CREATIVITY	EVIDENCE OF TASK COMMITMENT
• logical & analytical thinking	• Bodily-kinesthetic				
• quick to see patterns & relationships	• Interpersonal				
• understands complex concepts & abstraction	• Intrapersonal				
• quick mastery of information	• Linguistic				
• grasps underlying principles	• Logical - Mathematical				
• likes intellectual challenge	• Musical				
• jumps stages in learning	• Naturalist				
• problem—finds and problem—solves	• Spatial				
• reasons things out for self					
• formulates & supports ideas with evidence					
• can recall a wide range of knowledge					
• independently seeks to discover how and why of things					
• concern for justice, moral & ethical issues					
• sensitivity & empathy					

INDIVIDUAL PROFILE FOR _____

MEANS OF IDENTIFICATION: ....

....

LEARNING NEEDS: ....

....

....

SUGGESTED PROVISIONS:
WHAT

WHEN/WHERE

....

RECORD OF PROVISIONS:

UNIT ANALYSIS AND ADAPTATION

When using an existing unit or writing a new one, you can ask the following kinds of questions to ensure that children with special abilities will be challenged and motivated to learn. If at least some of the elements can be incorporated, that is an excellent start.

1. SHOULD THERE BE A HIGHER LEVEL ACHIEVEMENT OBJECTIVE OR SKILL OBJECTIVE ADDED?

The answer will not always be "yes". Often an objective is broad enough to allow scope for very able children. Sometimes though, a higher level content objective can be added for a group of children with special abilities or a separate objective based on a particular skill e.g. an independent learning one.

2. ARE A RANGE OF ABILITIES AND MULTIPLE INTELLIGENCES BEING CATERED FOR IN THIS UNIT?

In every unit, every type of ability cannot be catered for, but you can ensure that a range is being catered for by including a variety of activities and different ways of responding.

3. DOES IT ALLOW FOR DEPTH OF THINKING SUCH AS EXPLORATION OF CONCEPTS, THEMES, ISSUES, CROSS-CURRICULUM IDEAS?

Complexity and abstraction and a chance to explore ideas in depth are needed rather than just knowledge and skill acquisition.

4. ARE THERE NEGOTIABLE / CHOICE ELEMENTS, OR IS EVERYONE IN THE CLASS EXPECTED TO DO THE SAME?

Levels of independence and ability can be catered for through choice. Activities could be open-ended so that responses can be made in various ways.

5. COULD SOME PARTS BE COMPACTED TO ALLOW FOR EXPLORATION OF INTERESTS?

If determining prior knowledge shows that some children have already mastered some content or skills, allow them to choose areas of interest to explore. Prior knowledge can be gauged through: pretesting, discussion, brainstorming, diagrams, what I know / what I'd like to find out sheets, information from parents.

6. ARE CREATIVE PRODUCTS POSSIBLE?

Products, which can include performances, should be able to be original, not all the same.

7. DOES THE UNIT ALLOW FOR INDIVIDUAL PACE?

This may mean working through material at a faster pace allowing more time to explore something in-depth.

8. DOES THE UNIT ALLOW FOR AN APPROPRIATE LEVEL OF INDEPENDENCE?

As outlined earlier, children can work at varying levels of independence. It is frustrating to be held back when you have good ideas of your own to pursue.

9. IS SELF-ASSESSMENT INCORPORATED?

This may be through setting and evaluation of own goals or using preset criteria and self assessing against those.

10. IS THERE ANYTHING IN THE UNIT THAT IS MOTIVATING TO GIFTED UNDERACHIEVERS?

This may mean allowing for choice, interests and different ways of responding and having a real purpose for a study.

11. IS THERE THE POSSIBILITY OF MOBILITY IF NECESSARY?

This may entail working outside of the classroom or even the school at times.

12. IS THERE ANY CONSIDERATION GIVEN TO THE SOCIAL AND EMOTIONAL NEEDS OF CWSA?

This may be directly through inclusion of particular topics or indirectly through using some of the suggestions that follow.

SOCIAL/EMOTIONAL DEVELOPMENT

No one can make you feel inferior without your consent

Eleanor Roosevelt

This is great advice but usually not realised until adulthood. Surprising to many, is the fact that gifted children often do feel inferior because inferiority equates to difference or being rejected, of not being part of the popular or 'in' group.

What can the teacher do to enhance social / emotional development? The answer is:

RESPONSIVE ENVIRONMENT RESPONSIVE ENVIRONMENT RESPONSIVE ENVIRONMENT!!!

A POSITIVE TEACHER ATTITUDE

The most important thing is your attitude. Show you like this child. Try not to use words like *over* sensitive, taking things *too* seriously or being *too* idealistic. Emotional giftedness is not *too much*; it is emotional depth and intensity. Gifted children not only think differently from their age peers; they can also feel differently.

▸ **Recognise that children may be extroverts or introverts** – one is not better than the other; it is a different personality style. Extroverts learn and think by talking with others, they like to share ideas, answer quickly, do not hide their feelings, are spontaneous and like to have many friends. Introverts process ideas internally and may not want to share them, are very private people, need time alone, are very reflective, probably have a few special friends and may feel lonely in large groups of people.

▸ **Remember children with special abilities don't have to act "gifted" all the time** – they are children. It is hurtful to use their ability against them such as "If you're so smart, why can't you tie your shoelaces?" or "You might be in the enrichment class but you can't be that smart if you don't know this". A child can talk eloquently during the day about various theories of why dinosaurs became extinct but might still need to sleep with "blankie" at night.

▸ **Don't allow other children to use "put down" language.**
We don't allow racial slurs or name-calling for those with disabilities so why turn a blind eye to "nerd" and worse for gifted children?

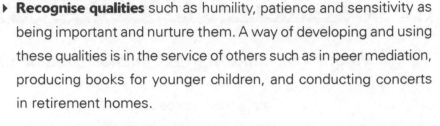

> **Recognise qualities** such as humility, patience and sensitivity as being important and nurture them. A way of developing and using these qualities is in the service of others such as in peer mediation, producing books for younger children, and conducting concerts in retirement homes.

> **For some children, leadership increases their self esteem** and also allows an outlet for service to others. It may be leadership of younger children, teaching new skills to the class such as in art or leading a special cultural group. However, not all children with special abilities want to be leaders. There are also different forms of leadership, some of which is quiet and behind the scenes, rather than up front. Learning about leadership is also worthwhile with such content as conflict resolution, problem–solving, planning and studying the qualities of leaders.

> **As these children may be intellectually capable** of understanding adult humanitarian issues and feel the weight of the world on their shoulders, they need outlets to do something or they feel powerless. Thus, real community projects and studying real issues need to be part of their curriculum.

... real community projects and studying real issues need to be part of their curriculum.

> **Conceptual learning also contributes** to emotional development through the discussion of such concepts as prejudice, sensitivity, persistence, power. It helps children to develop awareness of their own values and the values of others. Discussing quotes such as the one from Eleanor Roosevelt on the previous page can help children to develop insights about themselves.

> **Like-ability grouping is necessary some of the time**. Children with special abilities need to interact with others of similar ability so that they do not always feel different, so they can form friendships as well as for intellectual stimulation. These groups may be mixed age at times. It may allow them opportunities to find true peers. Peers are not always the same age; it is more to do with a person to whom you are drawn, with whom you have something in common, who understands you and accepts you.

> **Adult mentors who accept gifted children** and are interested in them can also help them to view their difference as positive rather than negative. A mentor who shares a strong interest with a child can help the child to see that it takes time to develop skills to a professional level, thus relieving the pressure to perform perfectly

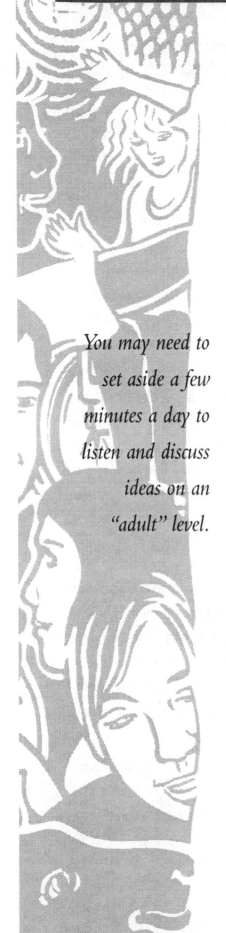

You may need to set aside a few minutes a day to listen and discuss ideas on an "adult" level.

without practice. Mentors can help children to strive for excellence, not perfection. A mentor of one's own ethnic group and gender can be powerful.

▸ **Recognise that when a child challenges** you, it may be their strong sense of justice coming to the fore. Don't be upset by it or see it as defiance; give your reasons for what you did or said. Even be prepared to admit you were wrong occasionally! Sometimes humour (not sarcasm) can defuse a situation also.

▸ **Listening to them may be particularly important** for some children with special abilities if other children in the class do not share their interests. You may need to set aside a few minutes a day to listen and discuss ideas on an "adult" level.

▸ **Be prepared to learn from them or with them**. Some children will know more than you do about certain things. Remember they don't know all that you know and they won't have as much wisdom as you do about the world but they might have a passion area that they know an enormous amount about. Let them share that passion with you.

▸ **Acknowledge and value their strengths**. For instance if a child is good at thinking up original ideas, orally articulate and good at art but has difficulty with reading and writing, put most emphasis on the strengths, not the deficits. Think where you get your self-esteem – from the things you are good at. No one wants someone always showing them how poor they are at things. If developing an IEP, use it not to focus on deficits, but first and foremost to develop abilities and interests further.

▸ **Allow creative outlets** for expressing feelings like personal diaries, painting, poetry, drama and music.

▸ **Practise reflective listening** so that you reflect back to the child their concerns without stating any judgment. This often lets the child open up more and elaborate because you are showing that you are listening. Acknowledging their feelings does not necessarily mean agreement.

▸ **Allow the child to engage in role play** in a small group situation. This may include communication skills, assertiveness training and social skills.

Give them the big picture.

▸ **Facilitate personal growth plans**. The child thinks about:

— Something I would like to change or develop.

— A goal based on this.

— What are the roadblocks to get around?

— Who are the people who will help?

— What are the steps I'll take?

— How am I managing on each step?

▸ **The Creative Problem-Solving process** outlined earlier (p.16) for staff problem–solving can also be used for individuals or groups of children. If there is a personal problem such as "no one likes me. I don't have any friends" or a group problem such as "kids call us nerds because we're in the enrichment group" then the six–step process can be worked through so that solutions are found.

▸ **Allowing children to learn cognitively** in a variety of ways, choosing their own preferred way when learning new material or carrying out something in depth, contributes to emotional development through acceptance of individuality. For example, if a child learns well visually and spatially, let them see what needs to be done. Give them the big picture. Let them visualise the end product or let them watch someone else perform the task. Allow movement and hands-on learning for a kinesthetic learner. Create chances for a verbal child to talk, for a musical child to create or listen to music, for a naturalist to engage with natural topics and classify, for someone who thinks logically and scientifically/ mathematically, to reason and experiment. Remember some children like to (even need to) learn with others, work in a group, discuss ideas. Others prefer to work alone and reflect on what they are doing.

Most of these suggestions can be carried out in the classroom. Some are planned strategies; others are just ways of interacting with very able children. Some could be facilitated in a wider school context when appropriate such as mixed age group role play, leadership activities and working on real issues.

RELATING TO PARENTS

What parents most dread is the "brick wall syndrome". They just want to be listened to and their knowledge about their children recognised. If a parent arrives and says her/his child is very able but seems to be a little bored or unhappy at school, you could:

- be defensive
- fight back
- see it as a slur on you

OR

- listen
- keep an open mind.

> ▸ Understand what the parents may have experienced such as meeting brick walls earlier, being labelled as pushy, seeing their child unhappy through teacher attitude or peer ridicule, having their child's abilities seen as an inconvenience in the school, being kept on their toes constantly by a child who from an early age has always been on the go, thirsting for knowledge.

> ▸ Agree to observe closely and get back together.

> ▸ Provide specific assessment data. Ask the parents to provide specific information such as examples of what their child says, makes, writes or paints, questions they ask, interests, how they choose to spend their recreational time.

> ▸ Develop some shared goals.

> ▸ Report on positives; don't just wait for negatives.

Parents want what is best for their children. The offer of partnership is music to their ears. Working co-operatively with families ultimately benefits THE CHILD.

What parents most dread is the "brick wall syndrome".

CONCLUSION

Concepts of special abilities are wide and include a range of abilities valued in different cultures. Potential as well as achievement should be considered.

Children with special abilities can be provided for in the regular school setting if the environment is inclusive of diversity and all needs and if attitudes are positive. A responsive environment contributes to identification and appropriate programming.

Identification is multi-method and is most effective when it is school-wide and includes family input. Identification of abilities leads to identification of needs which suggest the programming needed.

Children who are gifted and talented have both cognitive and affective needs. They may think and feel differently than many of their age peers. You, as a teacher or principal, can make a huge difference to their learning and happiness. Positive teacher attitude is vital for their social, emotional and cognitive development.

A written policy can mean on–going commitment. Policy development needs to be preceded by discussion of philosophical isues about who cwsa are, what their needs are, why they should be provided for. As a school, you can analyse what you are already doing (using techniques outlined in Section 2), decide what you could do and put these together in a policy. A person or people to co-ordinate implementation of policy is desirable.

Differentiation incorporates acceleration and enrichment. Children with special abilities don't need more practice; they need less. AVOID MORE OF THE SAME!

Differentiation of content, process, product and environment allows abilities to be further developed. This can occur in the wider school environment and by adapting units of work in the classroom. People from outside the school may be involved as mentors at times.

Strategies can include discovery of patterns and principles, higher level thinking which applies knowledge, independent contract learning, producing creative products, conceptual learning, studying real issues and creative problem-solving. Teachers can facilitate this by compacting time spent on the basics, allowing for flexible grouping and chances for discussion, facilitating rather than telling, teaching independent learning skills and negotiating learning contracts.

A teacher who creates a responsive environment which caters for social, emotional and cognitive needs allows cwsa to enjoy learning in his/her classroom. If there is also a responsive environment in the school, you can make every year a good year for children with special abilities.

> *Children with special abilities don't need more practice; they need less.*

One can never consent to creep when one feels the impulse to soar

(Helen Keller)

LET'S HELP OUR GIFTED AND TALENTED CHILDREN TO HAVE THAT IMPULSE AND WATCH THEM SOAR!

RECOMMENDED READING FOR CHILDREN

Below is a list of just a few books which may appeal to able children on an emotional level.

PICTURE BOOKS FOR YOUNG CHILDREN

A Bit of Company by Margaret Wild (1991)

Amazing Grace by Mary Hoffman (1991)

Communication by Aliki (1993)

Chrysanthemum by Kevin Henkes (1991)

Dragon Quest by Allan Baillie (1997)

Ebb's New Friend by Jane Simmons (1998)

Feelings by Aliki (1984)

Henry and Amy by Stephen Michael King (1998)

The Most Wonderful Egg in the World by Heine Helme (1983)

The Paperbag Prince by Colin Thompson (1992)

The Snow Lambs by Debi Gliori (1995)

The Very Best of Friends by Margaret Wild (1989)

The Whale's Song by Dyan Sheldon (1990)

Wilfred Gordon McDonald Partridge by Mem Fox (1984)

NOVELS FOR YOUNG READERS

Biddy Alone by Wanda Cowley (1988)

Catwings by Ursula Le Guin (1990)

Charlotte's Web by E B White (1963)

From the Mixed - up Files of Mrs Basil E Frankweiler by E L Konigsburg (1967)

Homesick, My own Story by Jean Fritz (1987)

Hugo and Josephine by Maria Gripe (1962)

Mouse Time by Rumer Godden (1995)

Much Ado About Aldo by Johanna Hurwitz (1978)

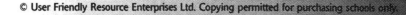

My Father's Dragon by Ruth Stiles Gannett (1948)

Shadrach by Meindert de Jong (1957)

The Butterfly Lion by Michael Morpurgo (1996)

The Chalk Box Kid by C Bulla (1987)

The Chicken Gave it to Me by Anne Fine (1992)

The Shrinking of Treehorn by Florence Parry Heide (1975)

PICTURE BOOKS FOR OLDER CHILDREN (8-9 YEARS UPWARDS)

Arabella by Wendy Orr (1998)

Ernest and Ethel by Raymond Briggs (1998)

How to Live Forever by Colin Thompson (1995)

Looking for Atlantis by Colin Thompson (1996)

Rose Blanche by Christophe Gallaz (1996)

Stormy Night by Michele Lemieux (1999)

The Lost Thing by Shaun Tan (2000)

The Silver Pony by Lynd Ward (1973)

The Staircase Cat by Colin Thompson (1998)

Tower to the Sun by Colin Thompson (1997)

Voices in the Park by Anthony Browne (1999)

Way Home by Libby Hathorn (1994)

Weslandia by Paul Fleischman (1999)

BOOKS FOR OLDER READERS (10 +):

A Cage of Butterflies by Brian Caswell (1992)

A Time to Fly Free by Stephanie Tolan (1983)

A Wrinkle in Time by Madeleine L'Engle (1962)

Bridge to Terabithia by Katherine Paterson (1978)

Come Sing, Jimmy Jo (1985)

Dreamslip by Brian Caswell (1994)

Fat Four Eyed and Useless by David Hill (1987)

Holes by Louis Sachar (1998)

Just Juice by Karen Hesse (1998)

Out of the Dust by Karen Hesse (1997)

Stone Fox by John Reynolds Gardiner (1980)

The Lottie Project by Jacqueline Wilson (1997)

The Music of Dolphins by Karen Hesse (1996)

The Outside Child by Nina Bawden (1989)

Underrunners by Margaret Mahy (1992)

Older children often like to read biographies and autobiographies. These can be of people past or present from a variety of cultures. Reading about these people who have made recognised contributions to society can contribute to self-understanding.

BOOKS WRITTEN ESPECIALLY FOR GIFTED CHILDREN

Adderholdt-Elliot, Mariam (1987) Perfectionism: *What's bad about being too good?* MN: Free Spirit

Delisle, James and Galbraith, Judy (1987) *The gifted kids survival guide II* (for ages 11-18). MN: Free Spirit

Galbraith, Judy (1987) *The Gifted Child's Survival Guide (for ages 10 and under).* MN: Free Spirit

Galbraith, Judy (1992) *The gifted child's survival guide (for ages 11-18).* Victoria: Hawker Brownlow

Hipp, Earl (1985) *Fighting invisible tigers. A stress management guide for teens.* MN: Free Spirit

* EXPLANATION OF ANCIENT EGYPTIAN MULTIPLICATION:

Numbers in left column are doubled.

Numbers in right column are halved and remainders left out.

Whenever the numbers in the right column are even, the row is crossed out.

To find the answer, the numbers not crossed out in the left column are added together.

REFERENCES

Bevan-Brown (1996) Special abilities : A Maori perspective. In D McAlpine & R Moltzen (Eds) *Gifted and talented. New Zealand perspectives.* Palmerston North: ERDC, Massey University

Bloom, B (1956) *Taxonomy of educational objectives : The classification of educational goals. Handbook 1: Cognitive domain.* NY: Longmans, Green and Co.

Clark, B (1997) *Growing up gifted. 5th edition.* New York: Merrill

Davis, G & Rimm, S (1994) *Education of the gifted and talented. 3rd edition.* Needham Heights, MA: Allyn & Bacon

Education Review Office (1998) *Working with students with special abilities.* Education Evaluation Report No 3 Autumn 1998

Gardner, H (1983) *Frames of Mind - the theory of multiple intelligencies.* London: Heineimann

Goleman, D (1996) *Emotional intelligence: Why it can matter more than IQ.* London: Bloomsbury

McAlpine, D & Reid, N (1996) *Teacher observation scales for children with special abilities.* NZCER & ERDC, Massey University

Maker, J & Neilsen, A (1995) *Teaching models in education of the gifted. 2nd edition.* Austin, TX: Pro-Ed

Ministry of Education (2000) *Gifted and talented students: Meeting their needs in New Zealand schools.* Wellington: Learning Media

Piechowski, M (1997) *Emotional giftedness: An expanded view.* Apex 10 (1), p37-47

Ramos-Ford, V & Gardner, H (1997) <u>Giftedness from a multiple intelligences perspective</u>. In N. Colangelo & G. Davis (Eds) Handbook of gifted education. 2nd edition. MA: Allyn & Bacon

Renzulli, J & Reis, S (1985) *The schoolwide enrichment model : A comprehensive plan for educational excellence.* Mansfield Centre, CT: Creative Learning Press

The quotations from Eleanor Roosevelt and Helen Keller were cited in:
Winebrenner, S (1992) *Teaching gifted kids in the regular classroom.* MN: Free Spirit

Acknowledgments

Braid, Christine and Fraser, Nikki for their valuable advice on children's literature